COPYRIGHT NOTICE

DEDICATION

This book is dedicated to Nurse Practitioners, Physician Assistants, Entrepreneurs, and Physicians who want to open a private practice mental health clinic.

CONTENTS

INTRODUCTION

Have you been struggling with the process of opening a mental health private practice clinic? Are you searching the internet or meeting colleagues with their practice who are giving you information here and there without much information? If you do not know where to start, this book is for you. I opened a mental health private practice clinic without having a blueprint. I made several costly mistakes that you do not have to. If you are thinking of opening your mental health private practice and do not know where to start, follow the process outlined in this book as a guide. Results may vary for everyone.

01 Register Your Business

Company Registration Process

- Appointment with CPA
- Business Form
- Business Name
- Register Business at State's Corporation Commission

Think about your business name. Do not make it complicated. Try to make it short and straightforward. You can use key terms that identify with your **niche** or population in Psychiatry. It may be beneficial to add keywords like Psychiatry or Mental Health Clinic in your business name if allowed by your state. Few examples are T and J **Addiction Family** Clinic (serving all ages struggling with substance abuse) and Trinity **Maternal** Psychiatry (serving women during pregnancy and postpartum). Using key terms may help patients locate you quickly on the map or Google.

Next, consult your Certified Public Accountant (CPA) on the best type of business form and structure for you. Ask your CPA about the advantages and disadvantages of each. There are several types of business organization forms: Sole Proprietorship, Partnership, Limited Liability Company (LLC), Professional Limited Liability Company (PLLC), and Corporations. Business structure can be an S corporation (tax paid on income by owner) or a C corporation (taxed separately from the owner). The registration can be done online or in-person at your State's Corporation Commission that creates LLCs. Most of the time, it can be approved the same day or take a few days to weeks. Your state may require a Statutory Agent or a person who will accept legal documents, such as a lawsuit notification on your business's behalf. If you wish to expand beyond your state, you can apply to your preferred state as a Foreign LLC. Start working on the logo for your business.

DAY 02 Secure The Location

Securing your location can mean different things. In this book, secure your location means to start with searching around the zip code in the area you want to open your mental health clinic. For example, you can begin by searching with key terms: Psychiatrists by zip code 85244, Mental Health Clinics near zip code 85224, and Mental Health Organizations in 85244. Once you get a list, look up what they offer and see if it is like what you plan to offer. Next, search for properties in the preferred location to rent or purchase if you can. If you plan on seeing patients via Telehealth, you will need a virtual office. I suggest getting a virtual office with access to a physical office; you can see patients if you need to, especially if you plan to give controlled substance prescriptions.

Due to COVID-19, prescribing controlled substances without seeing the patients in person initially has been relaxed by the Drug Enforcement Administration (DEA). However, this may reverse once the COVID pandemic improves or resolves. Please refer to https://www.deadiversion.usdoj.gov/fed_regs/rules/2019/index.html for more updated information

DAY 03-04 Secure a Property or Office Space

Schedule an appointment with Property Managers or a Realtor in charge of the office space you want to purchase or rent. Try to narrow the properties you want to look at based on your budget. If you plan on doing Telehealth only, you will need a psychical address to access a mailbox. Initially, most insurance companies' payments will be checks mailed out to you before it becomes an electronic deposit. The last option may be more cost-effective.

Psychiatric offices do not need much to start if you are on a low budget. A waiting area with 1-2 offices to see patients, a strong internet connection, and 1-2 computers are the major items you need to get started on a limited budget. Sign your lease or sign a purchase agreement. If you are purchasing, the Realtor may require that you have a pre-approval letter from your bank. If you are leasing or renting, the property managers/owners may require a deposit of your first and or last month's rent before moving in.

DAY 05 Obtain Employer ID Number

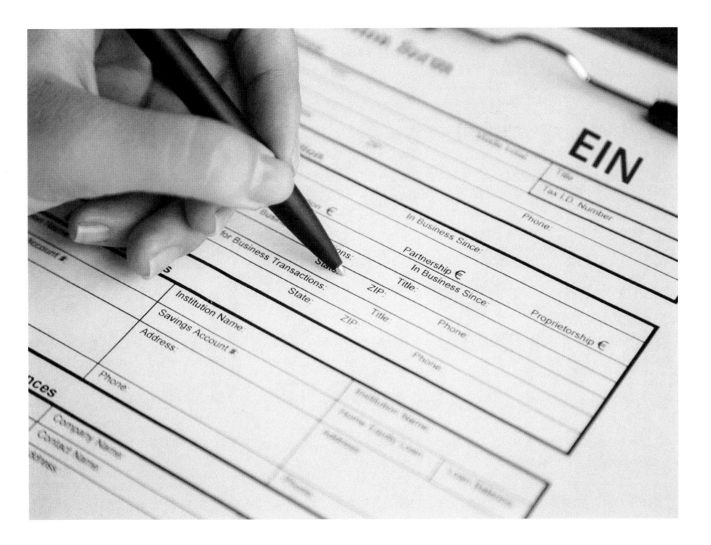

If your business name has been approved, go to IRS.gov, look for File. Under File, chose business and self-employed. Then click on Employer ID number (EIN). Once it opens, click apply of an EIN online. Once you have completed your EIN application, you will get a letter to download and save on your computer or email it to yourself. Please keep this document in a safe and secure place for future reference.

DAY 06 Open a Business Checking Account

Go to your bank and open a business account. Make sure you have your EIN letter or have easy access to it. The EIN will be needed to open your business account. You may also want to get a business credit card that you will need to use for your expenses and earn cashback.

Deposit your capital in the account that you will use to start your business. Pay all business-related costs through your business account from this point on. Make an appointment with your bank's credit card processing department or contact other card processors such as Square, Stripe, etc.

DAY 07 Clinic Policies and Procedures

Start working on your clinic Policy and Procedures. Things you may want to include in your policy but not limited to:

- Telehealth Policy
- Pre-registration/ Patient Demographics (name, DOB, driver's license #, phone number, email, medication allergies/reactions, gender, guardian information if a minor, reason for visit, current medications, previous Psychiatric Provider (s) including Therapists, General Practitioner, Hospitalizations)
- Release of information from medical records to be released from your organization or received from another organization. You can include Complete Medical Records, Laboratory Reports, Psychiatric Assessment, Psychological Report, Physician Progress Notes, e.tc. Also include name, signature, and expirations date on the form, and signature for someone in your organization to sign as a witness
- Authorization to Disclose Health Information to selected people (i.e., family, friends, spouse)
- Primary and secondary insurance information (patient's name and date of birth, policy holder's name and date of birth, insurance name, insured social security #, patient relationship: self, spouse, child, other.).
- Signature of patient or guardian
- Controlled substance policy and preferred Pharmacy information
- Clinic office hours, emailing, cell phone/Texting policies
- Answering Service
- Prescription refill requests
- Confidentiality statement
- Legal testimony
- Forms such as Short-term disability/FMLA/Letters completion and fees if any
- Payments/Financial Responsibility Policy
- No show/cancellation policy
- Consent for treatment with psychoactive medications.
- Women taking meds during childbearing years/pregnant/breastfeeding
- Informed consent for treatment to be signed by an adult patient and a guardian if a minor

08 Domain Registration and Website Building

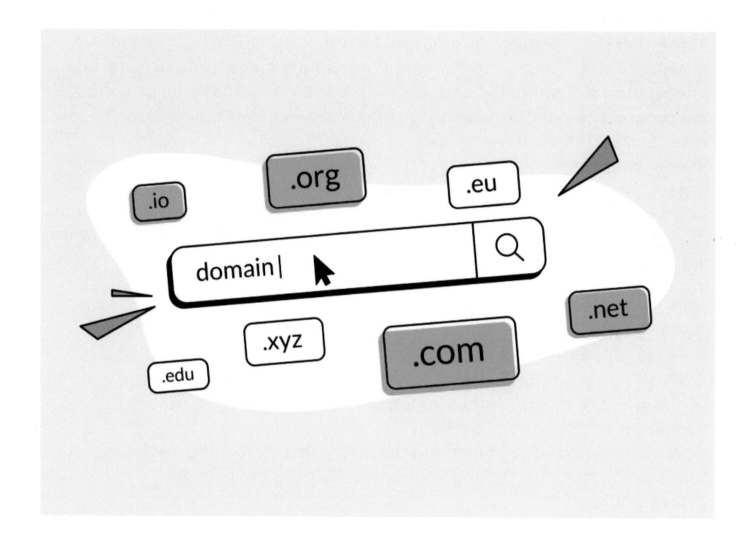

Register your business domain name and find a website hosting company if not part of the Domain you are using. Examples include Google Domains or GoDaddy, Namecheap, etc. You can work on building a website by yourself or outsource by hiring a web designer locally or abroad through companies like Pineapple Staffing and Feverr.com.

DAY 09 Business Email Registration

Create a business email that is HIPPA Compliant. Few organization examples are Hushmail, Google G Suite (will need to sign Business Associate Agreement (BAA) with Google), Microsoft office 365, etc. Paubox and Virtru can also be integrated to encrypt emails sent out of your organization's email in a fully encrypted and HIPAA compliant way. Keep your email simple, short, and easy to remember. I personally love Google G Suite because it comes with Google My Business, which can market, create ads, upload pictures, and target specific areas. I will speak further about this in detail under marketing tips.

DAY 10 Phone/Fax/Text Messaging System

O btain a phone line and a fast-paced internet connection. If you plan to see patients in several states via Telehealth, try to get a toll-free number. A landline through a local phone/internet company is ok. However, virtual phone lines through Voice over Internet Protocol (VoIP) phone line delivered over your internet connection may be better. There are several of them out there. Examples are RingCentral (need to sign a BAA), Velantro, Phone.com RingRX, etc. Most come with Fax and text messaging. You can use it to get incoming and outgoing Fax in addition to sending a text to your patients and staff.

Electronic Medical Records (EMR) Selections Process

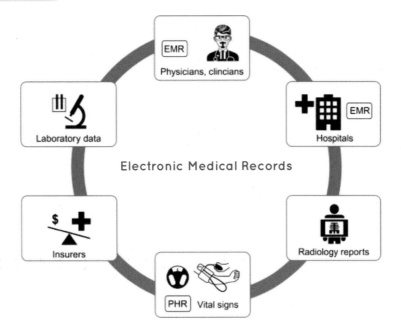

Start sampling of electronic medical records (EMR). Plan and write any questions you have. No question is stupid. There are a lot of great EMRs out there. It depends on your preference. Common EMRs for Psychiatric Practice are ICANotes, ChARM, AdvancedMD, Simple Practice, drchrono EMR, Practice Fusion, Athenaheath, Valant, Kareo, eClinicalWorks, PrognoCIS, ChartLogic, etc. Schedule appointment with chosen EMR vendor and ask questions such as:

- **Scheduling:** Can patients request to be scheduled from their portal or through my website (integrated with EMR)?

- **Form Completion:** Can patients complete their paperwork electronically? Can it be uploaded to the patient's chart? After completion, can certain information be transferred into the provider's notes?

- Can the Calendar remind patients about their appointments via text or email?

- **Charting:** Have the vendor show you how to complete a prescriber's intake/new patient assessment and a follow-up/progress note. Make your choice based on user friendly or what is suitable for you.

- **Billing:** If I choose to accept insurance, can billing be done by another organization or me directly in my EMR?

- **Clearinghouse:** What clearinghouses can be integrated with the EMR to transmit claims?

- Can claims or explanation of benefit (EOB) from the insurance company be posted automatically in the patient's account?

- **Lab Orders:** Can I send labs directly from my EMR? Can I receive lab results directly in my EMR?

- **Finances:** Can payments be processed within the EMR?

- **Telehealth**: Is there a built-in Telehealth in the EMR? If so, what is the cost?

- **Contracts:** Once I sign up, if I do not like the EMR, can I leave at any time, or will I be bound to a contract for 1-3 years? If I hire someone in my practice, but they leave earlier than expected, will I be able to cancel their plan, or will I be required to continue making payments until the terms of their agreement end?

- **Patient Insurance Eligibility:** Can I check my patient insurance for eligibility in my EMR?

12 Credentialing Process

If you choose to accept insurance in your practice, at this point you can start the Credentialing Process of getting on insurance panels. Credentialing can be done for free by you, or you can pay someone else. Doing it yourself can be very time-consuming or lead to mistakes and errors if you have no clue on what you are doing.

Nurse Practitioner Babara C Phillips's DIY Credentialing website https://www.clinicianbusinessinstitute.com/offers/fo6cC9zt/checkout may help guide you and save you money or undue stress. Paying others to help with the credentialing process may save you time if done correctly. Price ranges from $100 per insurance plan to $5,000 for a few insurance plans depending on the organization. The most cost-effective organization that I found and have personally used for under $1,000 for all insurance plans allowed in my area is Zmedsolutions.net.

They are a one-stop-shop, meaning they can help with credentialing and billing and other things that you may need. Below is a sample checklist of items to gather before starting the credentialing process but not
limited to:

- Driver's License
- Your Collaborative Practice Agreement with a physician if required by your state or profession.
- Your business information (Practice address and Practice mailing address (may differ from practice address)
- Type 1 NPI (each provider/prescriber in your practice)
- Type 2 NPI (your organization NPI). Apply in your NPPES portal with the user ID that you used to apply for Type 1. https://nppes.cms.hhs.gov/?userType=Provider#/
- Office phone number and Fax.
- Medical License
- State Certification Letter
- Updated Curriculum Vitae
- Copy of DEA Certificate
- Copy of Professional liability Insurance Certificate (should have your organization name). Berxi is very cost effective.
- IRS Documents (EIN Letter with Tax ID and Business name on it + W 9 Form)
- Voided check with business name and or Doing Business As (DBA) name if you have one.
- Your business account bank contact's name, address, phone number
- **Logins information to have on hand:** CAQH, NPPES Web Portal, PECOS Web Portal

Note: Credentialing can take 45 days to 6 months, sometimes a year for some insurance plans, depending on several factors. However, you can accept patients willing to pay with cash, HSA, FSA, Credit Cards etc.

DAY 13 Office Setup

Move into your office if you have not done so. Start furnishing it to your taste. Do not to break the bank. You can add and take away as you grow. Remember you will mostly likely increase, expand as needed, and or move.

- Continue working on your clinic Policies and Procedures
- Review and edit your website
- Create flyers, pens, business cards to use for marketing if you want

Flyers should include your business logo, the population you serve, services you provide phone, fax, email, insurances/payment system you accept, website, etc.
Pens should have business name, logo, phone, email address.
Business cards should include Provider's name, organization name, logo, phone/fax/email. Adding a place for appointment date and time on the back of the card may be beneficial.

DAY 14   Open House

Start planning for an open house by inviting Therapists, Social Workers from nearby Hospitals (especially Psychiatric Hospitals), primary care offices, and school Counselors if you are seeing children in your city or geographical area.

The open house may need to be virtual due to the COVID-19 pandemic. The purpose of the invitation is to let people know what you do, the opening date, services offered, pricing, and hours of operation. Allow enough time for questions and answers. Make sure you are ready to accept referrals and start seeing patients after your open house.

EMR, Clearinghouse Training, and Integration

Once you have chosen the best EMR and clearinghouse for your organization, request training. Practice, practice, and practice until you understand how to navigate through with little to no help. If you plan on billing, your chosen EMR may require a clearinghouse integration. The clearinghouse's job is to transmit electronic claims to the insurance carriers you accept after seeing patients.

The clearinghouse will scrub the sent claims for errors; if no errors, the claims will be securely transmitted electronically to the specified payer. The payer will accept or reject the claim, sending the status back to the clearinghouse, which then updates that claim's status in your portal. Rejected claims can be corrected in the clearinghouse portal and resubmitted back to the payer. Accepted claims will lead to a payer's reimbursement via check or Electronic Funds Transfer (EFT) along with an explanation of benefits (EOB) posted in the clearinghouse before the clearinghouse transfers it to your EMR. You should be able to post payers' payments in your EMR and notify patients if they owe you or need a refund.

Some EMR's have their clearinghouse already integrated or have contracted with a clearinghouse for billing. A sample EMR is Kareo. Several clearinghouses for psychiatric practice are Waystar/Navicure/ZirMed, Availity, Office Ally inc, TriZetto, etc.

Office Support Staff

Work on hiring office support staff in person or virtually, such as a Medical Assistant or a Nurse who can help answer phones, schedule or reschedule patients, help with vitals, injections, labs (onsite only), paperwork, prior authorizations, etc. The office support staff is a significant investment, even if you initially start a few hours a week. It will make your journey easier. Major hiring websites include Glassdoor, Indeed, etc. Furthermore, you will need to learn how to bill if you accept insurance or hire an in-house Biller. Outsourcing a Biller for a percentage is another option that can make your life easier. Ensure you understand how to monitor your claims in your chosen clearinghouse; if not, you run the risk of losing money.

Marketing

There are several ways to market your private psychiatric practice with or without a website. Several methods include but not limited to:

Psychology today

Psychologytoday.com is an excellent platform for Psychiatric practice advertising. If you have a friend or a colleague already on the platform, you can ask them to send you a referral link for you to sign up. Once you sign up and have a live account, you will have six months free of advertising. You can open several paid accounts and add up to three zip codes in your account following directions: Edit profile, then target listing. The zip codes should be in the states you are licensed to see patients.
Marketing Tip: Every 2-3 weeks, log into your account, and change zip codes to target other areas in your licensed states. The **rationale** for doing this is to reach as many patients as you can.

Google's My Business

Google My Business is another great way to advertise. You can target your listing by entering several cities you can service in your state, especially when seeing patients via Telehealth. You can promote events coming up or offer customers a deal. Patients can leave you a review on google that will help customers choose you over competitors.

Marketing Tip: You can upload pictures of the internal and external office, staff, e.t.c but save it like this: **Business Name_ Type of clinic_ City_ State**

For example:
Trinity_ Psychiatry_ Mental_Health_Clinic_ Dallas_Texas
Trinity_ Psychiatry_ Behavioral_Health_Facility_ Dallas_Texas

The **rationale** for saving your pictures like this, is that when people search for key words in your area, your practice may likely popup leading to them viewing your website and may lead to calls/appointment. You can also advertise your business on google using google ads. The cost varies but may be worth the investment.

Social Media

You can pay $10-$ 50 for advertising on social media like Instagram, Facebook weekly, or a specific period chosen. It is simple. If you cannot, please go to YouTube search and watch self-help videos like these:
"Instagram Ads Tutorial – How To Create Instagram Advertising Campaigns"
"Facebook Advertising - Learn How to Advertise on Facebook In Just a Few Minutes"
You can also outsource your social media ads.

Flyers/Pens/Business Cards

In the early weeks of opening your practice to quarterly after your practice is up and running, you can target Primary Care offices, Therapists, Psychologists, Urgent Cares, Pediatrician offices within 20-50 miles from your organization.

Marketing Tip: Schedule a brief meet and greet meeting with the organization staff, possibly during lunchtime. **Rationale:** It is always a great idea to put a face to the flyers, pens, and business cards that you drop off regularly. Meetings with the organizations may help the providers in the target organizations remember you or your staff when referring patients.

Word by mouth

If you and your staff provide good service to your patients and patients feel that you honestly care about them as a patient, they will refer their family, friends, and neighbors to your organization. They will also tell their other healthcare providers about your service.

Insurance Referral

Insurance will refer patients to you directly via provided email or give the patients a list to call you.

CONCLUSION

Treat your patients right and always do the right thing, no matter what. If the business does not work out in one area, try a different location or niche. Lastly, know that you can have the practice you have always wanted. All you must do is pray to God (if you believe) for direction, believe in yourself, work hard, and never give up.

Meet The Author

Dr. Christy Nneka Olloh is happily married to a loving and supportive husband, Emmanuel Olloh, for over twelve years. Together they have four beautiful children. She enjoys spending lots of time with family, learning new things, cooking, and traveling.

Her educational background started at Wake Technical Community College in Raleigh, North Carolina. She obtained a Degree in Nursing in December 2005. In 2011, she earned a Bachelor's Degree in Nursing from the Queen's University of Charlotte in Charlotte, North Carolina. She furthered her education at the University of Texas in Arlington, where she obtained a Master's Degree in Nursing with a Psychiatry specialization in 2015. In 2019, she completed a Doctorate in Nursing Practice. Dr. Olloh was inducted into the Nursing Honor Society while obtaining her Bachelor's and Master's degree.

Dr. Olloh has been in the Nursing profession for over 15 years. She currently practices in Maricopa Christian Psychiatry in Chandler, Arizona, as a Family Psychiatric Mental Health Nurse Practitioner. Dr. Olloh is licensed to assess and treat patients across the life span for Psychiatric Disorders, not limited to Anxiety, Depression, Attention Difficulty, Psychosis, and Bipolar disorders. Dr. Olloh also owns and operates GE Psychiatry and Consulting Services, LLC, to help healthcare professionals open successful clinics across the United States.

If you are struggling with your niche in Psychiatry practice? You are not sure which direction is right for you? Do you need help with running your open practice? Or you need Dr. Olloh to speak at your event?
Please contact Dr. Christy Olloh via email: called2BARN@gmail.com

For further information about Dr. Christy Olloh, visit the following websites:
https://www.mcpgpsychiatry.com

Made in the USA
Coppell, TX
04 June 2021